THE BIG PICTURE

S0-ARE-805

THRIFTY-

MURALS OF LOS ANGELES

The Big Picture

Photographs by Melba Levick
Commentaries by Stanley Young

A New York Graphic Society Book
LITTLE, BROWN AND COMPANY, BOSTON

For my Mother and my Father

Previous page: Cityscape by Terry Schoonhoven. *Right, from top:*
Unbridled by David Gordon; Estrada Courts mural; *Unity* by
Roderick Sykes. *Opposite:* Kent Twitchell's *Freeway Lady*

Acknowledgments

I would like to thank Stanley Young, without whose self-investment
and enthusiasm this book could never have been realized. For
taking the time to help me better understand the murals and their
creators I would like to thank Alonso Davis, Rozzel Sykes, Wayne
Healy, David Botello, Irma Nunez and Juan Gonzales. The fact that
Kent Twitchell believed in the project from its inception continually
reaffirmed my commitment and confidence. Also thanks to Deborah
Engleman who was so generous in sharing her knowledge and
information, to Sharon Ackerman for her advice, support and
companionship, and finally, my gratitude to all the artists, only a
portion of whom appear in this book. Their inspired work is the
reason for the existence of *The Big Picture.*

M.L.

Copyright © 1988 by Thames and Hudson Ltd, London

All rights reserved. No part of this book may be reproduced in any
form or by any electronic or mechanical means, including
information storage and retrieval systems, without permission in
writing from the publisher, except by a reviewer who may quote
brief passages in a review.

International Standard Book Number: 0-8212-1677-5 (hc)
0-8212-1671-6 (pb)
Library of Congress Catalog Card Number: 87-82617
First United States edition

New York Graphic Society books are published by
Little, Brown and Company (Inc.)
Published simultaneously in Canada by
Little, Brown & Company (Canada) Limited

Designed by Lawrence Edwards

PRINTED IN SINGAPORE

CONTENTS

INTRODUCTION

City of painted dreams

Los Angeles was destined to be the world center for contemporary murals.

It has a long tradition of painting its dreams in images and setting them out for the world to see. For what is a movie but a mural that moves?

Here, on the sandy backlots of film studios, armies of people fashion worlds and recreate epochs from bits of wood and glue; they design stage sets for film and television that dwarf humans. Angelenos are attuned to a certain sense of scale and imagination as far as art is concerned; the movies have always been bigger than life and twice as real.

It is a sense of scale that feeds the impulse to make murals, but it is the light that makes them visible. For 270 days a year, the bright Californian sun casts a light that murals adore. Colors that would be merely vivid in many climates are electrified in the bright daylight; exposed to the sun they jar the eye and make the murals scream.

The peculiar local sense of imagination also gave birth to flights of fancy such as Disneyland, itself a sort of three-dimensional moving cartoon mural. Angelenos are used to outrageous decoration. In a city where hot-dog stands are built to look like giant hot dogs and cars made to look like candy apples, the most flamboyant of murals know they are at home.

No one knows for sure just how many murals there are—several hundred "official" ones, of that we can be certain, and probably an equally large number of "unofficial" ones as well. None of them is more than eighteen years old, and the first were born in anger. In a city of images, the two largest minorities, the Chicanos and the Blacks, sought a violent restatement of their sense of self. They took to the walls to speak in the visual language of metaphor and expressed their sense of pride and community. On the walls of the *barrios* (Spanish for "neighborhoods") Mexican folk-images were translated through an American aesthetic based on billboards, comic books, cartoons and hard, graphic realism.

As the social unrest simmered down in the mid-seventies, the fires went out on the walls. The early murals remained, a faded but vibrant testimony to an era of self-discovery that had left an indelible stamp on the imagination of the city, and the tradition of mural art in Los Angeles was established. Politicians quickly recognized murals as inexpensive tools for community development—and an efficient means of keeping graffiti at bay in public places. The Citywide Murals Project was established in 1974 and some 250 murals added a strongly decorative element to the scene. With the Citywide Program, murals moved out of the ghettos (ethnic and artistic) and began to influence public life throughout Los Angeles.

Then came the ultimate recognition of the effects of murals on American culture: advertising billboards began to resemble murals. Walls were leased and five-storey-high portraits *without ad copy* appeared. The subjects, often well-known public sports personalities, were not smiling the omnipresent American smile, nor holding the omnipresent brandname product in their hand. These portraits simply did not have the look of a billboard about them; they were conscious works of art, in a realistic style, but painted and wordless. They were murals.

The tradition of commemorative murals was enhanced in 1981, when several large murals were painted in honor of the bicentennial of Los Angeles. In 1984, the Los Angeles Olympic Committee commissioned a host of giant murals to honor the 23rd Olympics, to be painted on downtown sections of the Freeway and by the Coliseum. The world marveled at these monumental works of art, and for the muralists who had been painting walls around Los Angeles for over a decade, it was a long overdue recognition. Murals have had to fight hard for their legitimacy.

Murals continue to sprout daily in Los Angeles. Downtown a professional muralist suspended in a giant electric scaffold paints a sports scene on the side of an eight-storey building, while in the Pico-Union area members of the Playboys gang stand on crates and ladders to paint the wall of a neighborhood market.

And they are everywhere in Los Angeles, these murals. They rise up from freeway off-ramps, appear in schoolyards, under bridges, unexpectedly on the sides of private houses. Most Angelenos have begun to take them for granted—a sure sign that they have become, by now, an established part of this city's appeal, like the long sand beaches, the cloudless skies, and the palm trees. For the visitor, the first-time tourist who takes nothing

7

The Streetscapers' *El Nuevo Fuego* was designed in 1982 with spaces left for athletes. Two years later came the scale-model with the athletes chosen. Lastly, the model was translated into the color-scheme for the next 6-foot-high section of wall to be painted

for granted, for readers of this book wherever they may be, these giant painted walls reveal themselves as astonishing decorations fit to grace a city that has always lived on image and fantasy.

Drawings and techniques

A lot of time is spent in the studio when the East Los Streetscapers design a mural. "As far as designing murals is concerned—well, there's always too many ideas," says Wayne Healy. The Payless Shoes Commission, *Corrido de Boyle Heights*, involved about eight months' designing, but since both Wayne and David Botello work full-time day-jobs they were only able to attack the mural for about eight man-hours a week.

Once the design is hammered out they make a 1 inch to 1 foot scale-drawing which serves as a blueprint. A color-cartoon is painted, cut into strips measuring the length of the portable scaffold by 6 foot high—the highest they can reach comfortably—and then covered over in plastic.

The wall is prepared by being scrubbed down. A cheap colour such as ultramarine blue or yellow ochre is added to the gesso-and-acrylic gel used to prime the surface. Although it is barely noticeable, this underlying shade tints the entire composition.

The strip of the color-cartoon for that day is divided into three, a third for each man on a scaffold, and the figures are outlined with a half-inch bristle brush. Botello takes care of the human provisioning, usually setting up a sunshade over the portable scaffolding and seeing an adequate supply of cold beverages is on hand in the cooler. They work a full day, but only on weekends or vacations.

On the ground the next morning, all the participants take a look at what they did the day before. They discuss corrections and alterations, then go up and make any necessary changes. Sometimes whole figures are revised or added during the painting once the composition begins to emerge on the wall.

The East Los Streetscapers use a variety of techniques that are unusual, such as sweeping lines and circles that break the composition into different color-sections, and strong foreshortening, reminiscent of the Mexican

muralists, which gives a sense of dynamic movement. "We've both done our homework," says Healy, referring to their study of the great Mexican muralists and the masters of western painting. They mention Rubens for his sense of movement, and Botello, especially, is taken with Van Gogh's color. Unexpected color-combinations are used to build up figures: a leg is made up of sweeping bands of white, yellow, blue, red and aqua, but no "flesh-tone" (p. 21).

A trademark of the Streetscapers is their use of colored lines, usually blues and indigos, to edge the forms in shadow and give an effect of reflected light. Sometimes pools of colored light pick out the figures in the mural as if they were lit on-stage. "The projected and reflected light adds an element of the environment without showing the source," notes Botello.

The Streetscapers murals are designed to be seen by two different kinds of viewer. They certainly have a formidable impact when seen at a distance from a speeding car, but they also contain elements like writing and small, detailed images that need to be seen close-up, by pedestrians on the sidewalk. The murals are meant to be read, and their symbols decoded.

At first glance one of the panels in *Chicano Time Trip* is an image of an attractive Spanish woman, but closer inspection reveals a burning Aztec temple. *La Española* concerns the domination of the indigenous peoples by the Spanish overlords—and ladies. Not all the images in the murals convey meanings, however. Some are just creations of pure fancy. "People still come up to us with their own explanations of what is going on in *Moonscapes* (p. 81). Some of them point out things we had never thought about, but it makes sense. Why not? Everyone can have their own interpretation."

Making the most of the space available to them is a challenge the Streetscapers enjoy. They let their figures over-run the area, whether on a wall 6 foot high or the side of a building of five stories. "We like to go off the edge." The most difficult assignment so far was not the massive 80-foot-square side of the Victor Building, nor the Department of Motor Vehicles, 10 feet by 500 feet, but a 6-foot-high wall that ran for 250 feet beside a gas station in East LA: "It was like designing a mural for a roll of paper-towelling," says Healy about *Filling Up On Ancient Energies* (p. 95).

Kent Twitchell took over one hundred and fifty photos of his sitter before he found the right pose for the *Gary Lloyd Monument*. Then he made seven portraits from the photo to get the one he used to make this master-cartoon, marked off into density/colour areas

Inside-outside

Kent Twitchell sees the wall first. Then he decides what he will do on it—that is, if he ever is allowed to paint a mural on the surface that has captured his heart: "It's very difficult to get a building you lust after." The Otis Parsons building where he painted his Master's project *Trinity* (p. 91) was one that had long excited his muralist's sensibilities, but he managed to secure it from the Los Angeles County Board of Supervisors only after lengthy negotiations—and at a price. "I had to promise my life away to get it." The building overlooking the Hollywood Freeway where he painted the "Freeway Lady" (p. 5) was obtained through the intercession of a well-known sculptor, and the underpass where Lita Albuquerque looks out over the Harbor Freeway (p. 23) involved him in protracted bureaucratic wrangling before the Californian Department of Transport gave permission. But not all buildings that arouse his passions prove so difficult. The wall for the *Ed Ruscha Monument* came into his hands by a fluke, and Steve McQueen (p. 113) was painted on a friend's house.

Even before he knows a wall is his, Twitchell runs through the repertory of images he has built up in his memory till he finds a suitable subject. Once he has permission to use the chosen building, he goes about getting the subject's co-operation. He approached Lita Albuquerque at Otis Parsons in Los Angeles where she had been teaching. Though Twitchell himself was teaching there, he had never met her. "I went over to her and said, 'I'd like to do a painting of you on a wall.'" Twitchell had his camera with him, took a few fast shots, and that was all she heard from him until she saw herself—larger than life—on the Harbor Freeway as part of the two-person *Seventh Street Altar Piece*. "It absolutely floored her. She had no idea it was going to be something that visible."

Ed Ruscha, on the other hand, was well aware of the extent of his proposed visibility. In 1978 Twitchell sent him a letter that was short and to-the-point: "Dear Ed Ruscha," it went, "To get right to it, I want to paint you on an exterior wall in downtown Los Angeles. I've secured a 5-story building near 10th and Hill, the old YWCA building. I would paint you standing alone, unsmiling, staring down at the viewers. The rest of the wall would be painted a dull blue-black, with nothing else on the wall." Twitchell enclosed an image of the wall cut from a 35 mm proof sheet, with the figure of Ruscha roughly sketched over it. Within the week Ruscha had agreed.

Once the wall and subject are fixed, there's the funding. Twitchell painted his early murals for nothing. His first "commercial" mural was *The Freeway Lady* (see Contents page). The County of Los Angeles and a matching grant from the National Endowment for the Arts provided enough money for materials and $153 *total* for the artist. The project took Twitchell six months.

Immediately after graduating from Otis, he secured a grant from the federal CETA program, providing him with $800 a month to do art in public places; later he won a competition from the Architect's Office in Sacramento, the California state capital, for a commission on a Department of Employment Office in Torrance, a suburb of Los Angeles. The *Ed Ruscha Monument* was originally funded with $4500 from the California Council for the Arts as a special Project, and

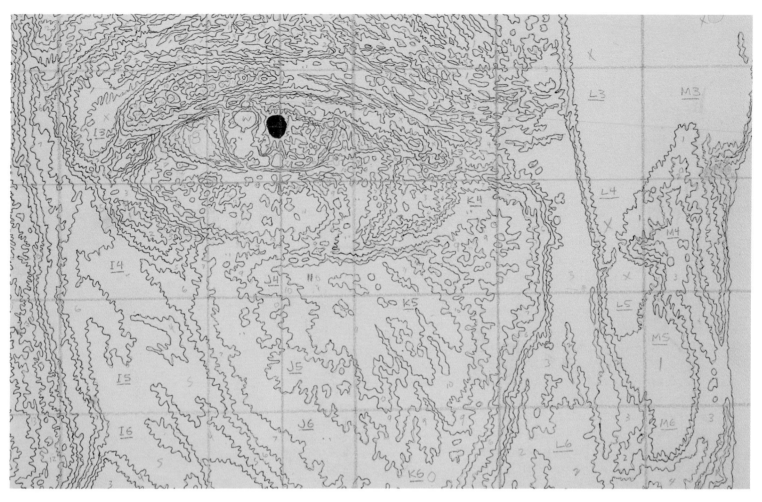

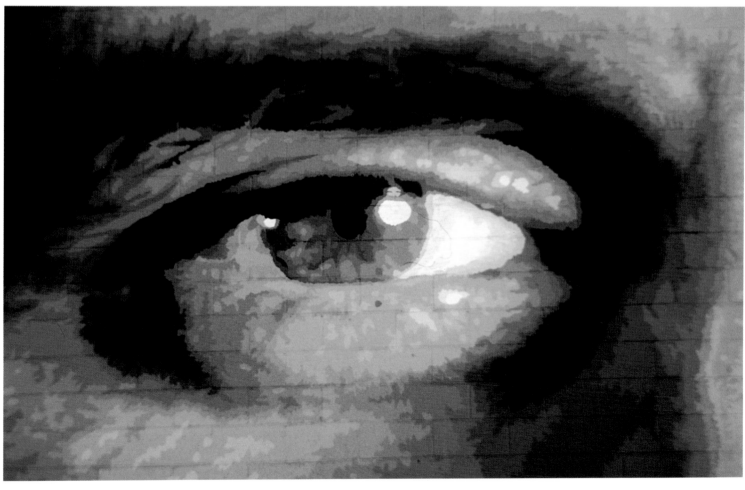

Above left: **the drawing for the** ***Gary Lloyd Monument*** **(see p. 93)**

Below: **A detail of a small oil portrait? In fact, a 4-foot-by-3-foot section of a 3-storey-high mural. Gary Lloyd's eye is 7,000 times larger than life**

recently—many years later—he received money from the 'National Endowment for the Arts for Art in Public Places Grant' to complete it.

Occasionally a private individual will approach Twitchell with both a space and money to complete a mural. This happened with the *Gary Lloyd Monument* on the side of City Sea Foods building in downtown Los Angeles (p. 93).

With access to the wall and funding, Twitchell turns to the creation of the mural. He takes around one hundred black and white fine-grain photos of the chosen sitter. For Gary Lloyd he took upwards of one hundred and fifty photos to capture the exact image he required— "strong but accepting, almost gestural."

He selects one negative which he prints several times, using a variety of different photographic papers to give a wide range of contrasts. Often he chooses a higher contrast "poster image" rather than the more naturalistic rendering. Using the single 8 by 10 black-and-white print as a model, Twitchell paints a detailed portrait in oils, in differing sizes, but never larger than life.

For some murals he has painted as many as seven different portraits of the subject before finding the one he sought. Twitchell was three-quarters of the way through the portrait of Ed Ruscha when he realized the facial expression was not what he wanted. In 1980, two years after shooting the original photos, he arranged with Ruscha for a second session. "This time I decided to use my studio where I could control the light." Ever since, Twitchell has used the same lighting for all his sitters: harsh, white, and from the side, throwing the face into sharp relief. The Ruscha mural ended up as a combination of the two photo sessions. The body and clothes are chosen from the early one, the head from the later.

Occasionally Twitchell paints the portrait in color, but for the most part he favors using black and white. "The different densities of the shades involved are easier to discern when the portrait is in black and white," he explains.

He divides a photograph of the portrait into a grid, each section corresponding to an area of wall 3 feet by 4 feet. The grid-section is blown up to an 8 by 10 print from which Twitchell makes a black-and-white cartoon.

breaking down the image as nearly as possible into its constituent light and dark areas. The resulting drawing (left) looks something like a relief-map of a rugged mountain range.

When he is content with the cartoon Twitchell photographs it, and projects a black-and-white slide on to a piece of market paper 3 feet by 4 feet. Using a soft graphite pencil he marks off the different areas of density.

In priming the wall, Twitchell uses a technique developed by his business partner, a paint chemist. If the wall is already painted, he sandblasts it. He hoses it down, and applies a 1:3 styrene acrylic-water mix on the damp surface. The acrylic is absorbed into the grain of the mortar or concrete, gaining purchase with countless tiny styrene roots. Once it is set, it is covered with a more concentrated coat of acrylic, applied by brush or roller, that bonds molecularly with the surface. Lastly, Twitchell covers the primed wall with a coat of titanium dioxide in a water-soluble acrylic base.

When he has found the center of his figure on the wall, Twitchell marks it with a vertical chalk-line, then starts drawing on the grids to left and right, beginning at the bottom and working upwards. He tapes on the 3 by 4 market paper sections with the cartoon in graphite, and traces the design through using a pressure-feed ball point pen able to work against gravity. Twitchell finds that the ball-point not only makes it easier to scribe the lines than a burnishing tool, but also makes it clear which of the myriad lines remain to be drawn.

The soft graphite leaves its mark clearly against the brilliant white surface. Twitchell immediately paints over the surface with a clear, water-based acrylic varnish. He began using varnish at this early stage to protect the delicate graphite lines, but then realized he had stumbled across an important time-saving step. "The brush just slides over the varnish," he explained. "I can paint twice as fast without the drag of the brush on a matt surface."

Once the line-drawing has been transferred and protected, Twitchell develops a palette of colors in his studio, mixing the paints meticulously and setting out the different values for each color in marked bottles. The color-range differs from mural to mural: the *Ed Ruscha Monument* was influenced by Caravaggio (the reds in the

Twitchell uses his van door as his palette; it's handy, and has the added benefit of sharing the same sun-exposure as the wall. At the bottom are the colors for Ed Ruscha's trousers and shirt. "The Ed Ruscha piece was influenced by the colors of Caravaggio, and Rembrandt—especially the flesh tones. But they've faded . . . "

shirt) and Rembrandt (the warm flesh tones). Twitchell is careful to use only triple 8 rated color pigments—the ones most resistant to fading in the harsh LA sun.

At the wall, he 'fine-tunes' his colors using the inside of his van door. "Sometimes I'll find that the line between two values of a color is too harsh, so I'll mix a half-value on the door. You're right there on the site; you've got exactly the same sun exposure." His van door is a palimpsest of the color-ranges of all the murals he has ever done. "On the door you can really play with the colors."

A mural may take anything from three months to finish (*The Freeway Lady*) up to one and a half years (*Ed Ruscha Monument*), counting just the time spent at the wall. Since he works on several murals at once, the time from start to finish may be much greater—as long as eight years for the *Ed Ruscha Monument.*

When the mural is completed, the wall is sealed with a coat of high-solids acrylic emulsion—that is, an acrylic resin which is chemically compatible with but slightly harder than the underlying acrylic paint.

Twitchell returns periodically to clean the mural and touch up any faded or damaged areas. Restoration and maintenance now takes up a good deal of his time, but murals are his life. "I never did murals as a prelude for getting into the galleries. I'm doing what I want to do and I'm going to keep on doing it." In early 1986 he turned down a $10,000 commission because it would have meant leaving Los Angeles for a few months, and taken him away from needed cleaning and repair.

Twitchell's figures are the visual equivalent of the prose of Hemingway. Uniformly, they lack gestures or emotions. They look out over the city with a frank,

unblinking gaze. "There are no expressions," he explains, "and this gives them a universality. My portraits are icons. I see them as monuments, like the stone figures on Easter Island."

Even when the image is five stories high, the attention to minute detail is unrelenting. The viewer can see every pore, every hair, on the hands of Ed Ruscha, even though they measure 9 feet from wrist to fingertip.

The result of Twitchell's vision and technique is evident. His murals do not portray idealized beings; they are actual people. Although painted on a monumental scale, they are accessible. They do not overpower. His figures keep watch over the vast city, softening and humanizing their environment, a sort of apotheosis of the ordinary.

On the scaffold and in the sling

"There were mornings when hitting the wall was hard," admitted Wayne Healy of the East Los Streetscapers. In a studio there is no freeway traffic roaring twenty feet below you, and you don't need to come down off the scaffold once an hour to breathe pure oxygen, as Judy Baca was obliged to do when painting her women's Olympics marathon mural beside a busy downtown off-ramp. You don't need to use a parachute-silk sunshade, or to keep a hat on all the time, or to wear mountaineers' sunglasses to keep the sun's reflection off the white gesso from making you go snow-blind.

You don't have to shin down a rope from five stories up when the power gets turned off, either, or take out one million dollars' worth of insurance because the owner of the parking lot gets nervous when he sees your half-ton

12

Right: Twitchell holds the master-cartoon for Ed Ruscha. *Far right:* His sling is dwarfed beside the unfinished hand. *Below:* Twitchell returns twice a week to work on the mural

Following pages: The *Ed Ruscha Monument*, downtown. "My pieces have to grow out of the ground, that's why I crop their feet. When there's something hidden, it makes them look bigger. There is a mystery involved."

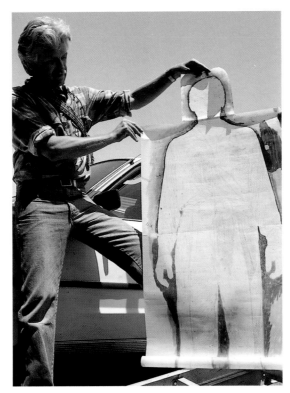

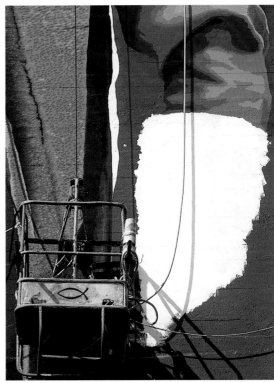

13

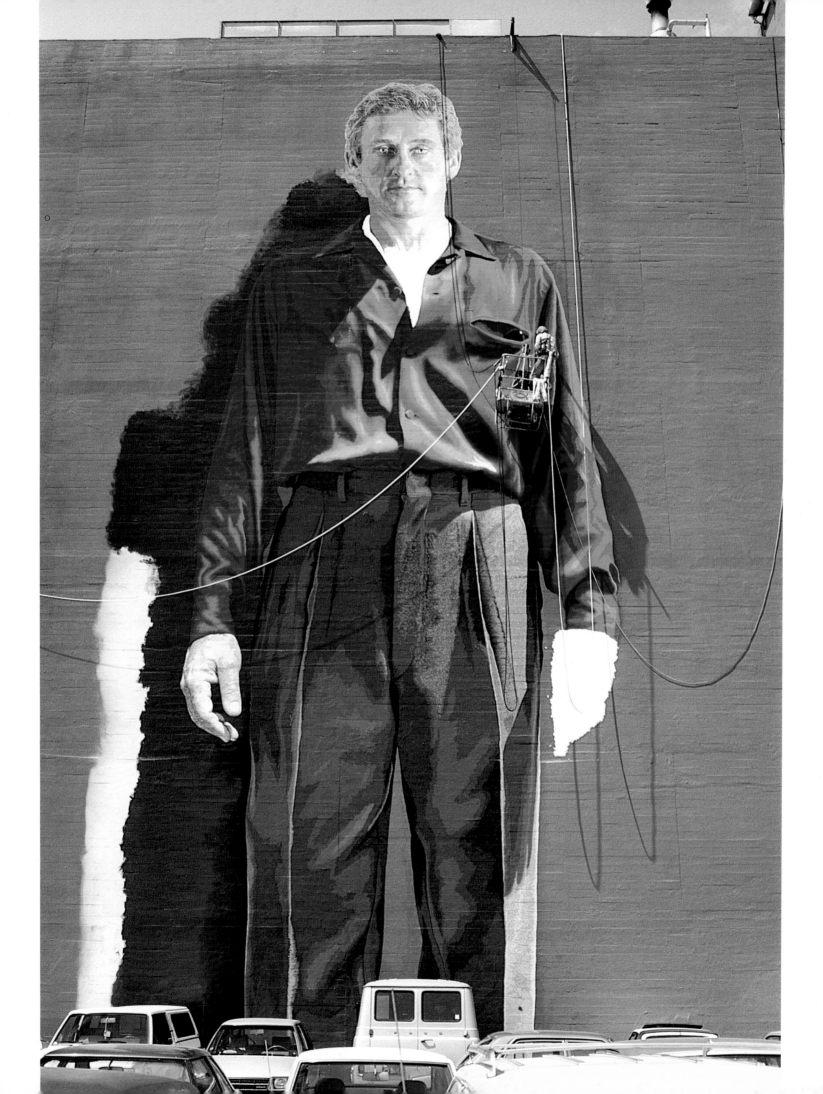

Kent Twitchell hitting the wall

stage begin to sway, four stories high above his customers' cars.

Just standing painting for twelve hours a day is demanding enough—working five stories up compounds the effort. "There's a lot of movement in the bucket, a lot of swing," says Twitchell. And every time he needs to move more than a dozen feet to either side, the limit of his reach from the sling, it's up to the top to grapple with the clamp on the parapet. And aging electric swings and stages have their quirks—if there's just a little precipitation, even misting, they give off shocks. Twitchell has to do exercises every day to stay fit for working outdoors, for "if I don't keep in shape, I really feel it at the wall."

"When you're up there on the scaffold, you're definitely a performing artist," says Wayne Healy. Pedestrians stop and ask you questions, or make suggestions; some are wary of a person who spends long hours all alone painting a wall for weeks on end.

Of course, there are areas in Los Angeles where it is the muralist who must be wary. Thomas Suriya remembers his apprehension at having to go out early each morning to work on his mural on Wilcox Avenue, around the corner from Hollywood Boulevard, "The Strip". At 5 a.m. the late-night traffic of transvestite prostitutes would just be yielding to the daytime assortment of shady characters. But he was soon an accepted regular on the block.

There are rewards for making art outside. A wall can become the site of a party or a town meeting. Neighbors bring food, youngsters join in and learn that painting is not a mystical process reserved for the solitary artist in his studio. "Collective murals break down the notion of individuality as the source of art," observes Vic Henderson.

Then, too, there is the feeling granted only to a muralist when, four stories below him a man stops, watches intently, and yells out, "Te aventaste!" David Botello translates this roughly as, "You've really flung yourself on that wall!" Of course the next day the same man may pass by again and shout only "Ya mero?", which means something like, "So, aren't you done yet?" Out on the streets you have to take the good with the bad.

David Gordon in front of his 600-foot-long mural *Unbridled*. It took him 13 months to complete, at a cost of $25,000

Biography of a mural

"They were modern Medicis," remembers Vic Henderson about the patrons who financed many of the murals in the early seventies. These were men who chose to invest in the creation of eccentric subject-matter in public spaces. They were art collectors who financed art they could not possess. Jordy Hormel, for instance, contributed $10,000 to fund the LA Fine Art Squad's masterpiece *The Isle of California*, a mural portraying a ravaged, post-cataclysmic Californian scene. "They were hip, wealthy people who were willing to risk their money. But they died along with the mural movement. . ."

After the flow of private funds had diminished muralists turned to a variety of official sources for funding. Their names read like an alphabet soup of institutions: CETA (Comprehensive Employment Training Act), CAC (California Arts Council), NEA (National Endowment for the Arts). At times it was non-governmental institutions such as SPARC (Social and Public Arts Resource Center) that funneled official funds to the individual artists.

In recent years, however, murals are once again attracting private patrons. Paul D. Harter has commissioned several murals from Chicano artists over the last decade, making the Victor Building (p. 100) a centerpiece for murals downtown. Donald Kanner offered Kent Twitchell funding and complete artistic freedom to undertake one of his "Los Angeles Artist's Monuments" on the wall of his downtown building City Sea Foods.

Unbridled (facing page) is a recent example of the confluence of an artists' determination, the involvement of a private patron, and the wholehearted co-operation of a civic institution. David Gordon had grown up in the beach area, and since childhood had had a recurring dream: that the horses in the historic Carousel on Santa Monica Pier came alive and were escaping. Gordon had learned the art of painting murals while working under Terry Schoonhoven, a member of the early LA Fine Arts Squad and one of the city's foremost muralists. He was determined to share his recurring vision with other people, and settled on an underpass in Santa Monica with a view of the Pacific Ocean to carry out his dream.

Gordon approached Frederick Weisman, a wealthy art patron, with plans for putting a mural of the escaping horses over an unfinished historical mural by Jane Golden. Her mural had not progressed past its initial phases for some years, and seemed unlikely ever to be completed. Weisman, however, was undecided about the project for some time, until Jacques Chirac, then mayor of Paris, came on a visit to Los Angeles.

Chirac had been responsible for helping revitalize public art in Paris, and Weisman sought the politician's advice on Gordon's mural project. Together they rode out to Santa Monica with the plans, looked at the site, and Chirac convinced Weisman that the idea was fantastic. . . and feasible. Gordon soon after received a $25,000 grant from the Frederick Weisman Foundation of Art to complete his mural.

Gordon had meanwhile been organizing community support for the project, and made a presentation to the forward-looking Santa Monica Arts Commission, the city institution responsible for all public art within its borders. The project was accepted, and Gordon began the mural in March 1985. He finished the 600-foot-long re-creation of his lifelong vision thirteen months later.

"*Unbridled* presents images that can be understood by anybody," notes Henry Korn, Executive Director of the Santa Monica Arts Commission. "The mural is a poignant metaphor for the cultural resurgence of this city, the reanimation of the historical structure. Our community of artists are our wild horses."

Details and colors

Murals have to fight for attention on the street with advertising billboards, their main competition, for both employ the same scale. They operate, however, in a very different manner. A billboard's message is purposely simplistic, with no need of the intricate detail which forms a part of many murals (over page).

And then there's the light: 270 days a year of hot, bright, sun. If a subtlety of shade cannot stand up to the sun, it is washed out, obliterated. The muralist who wants to make a powerful statement must accept the domination of light and choose colors that will survive at noon: reds, hot pinks, deep blues, bright yellows.

A contrast in styles
Above: Aztec motifs of a ceremonial boot and whimsical face grace a library wall, a detail from the mural *Ofrenda Maya. Above right:* a Toltec warrior's head dominates the side of El Chavo Restaurant in Hollywood. *Right:* Kent Twitchell's Botticelli-influenced Bride of *Bride and Groom*

A study in textures
Far left: the sculptured head of *Workers' Mural* struggles on stucco to express a political message. Twitchell's *Steve McQueen* surmounts the wooden projections of a bay window. An athlete in *Las Olimpiadas* gazes out from his concrete surface with the sad eyes of a Roman fresco. *Left:* Eloy Torrez' rendering of Anthony Quinn in *Pope of Broadway* has a variety of surfaces to contend with. The Streetscapers' massive leg of sprinter Valerie Brisco-Hooks pounds off a brick surface

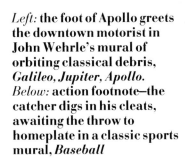

Left: the foot of Apollo greets the downtown motorist in John Wehrle's mural of orbiting classical debris, *Galileo, Jupiter, Apollo.* *Below:* action footnote—the catcher digs in his cleats, awaiting the throw to homeplate in a classic sports mural, *Baseball*

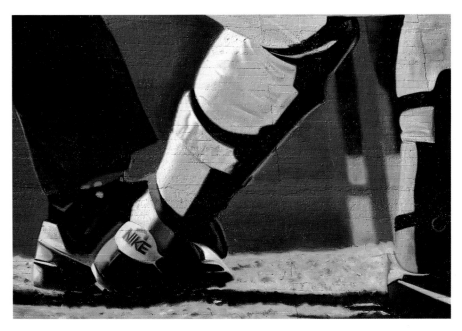

Twitchell washing two years of grime off Lita Albuquerque. His portrait, half of *Seventh Street Altar Piece*, is a true Angelano artpiece in its purest setting, for Albuquerque looks across 12 lanes of incessant freeway traffic to her counterpart, the portrait of artist Jim Morphesis (p. 26). "I draw artists because they're vulnerable, they put themselves out there to be judged," says Twitchell

Aging murals

Murals are not untouchable like works of art in a museum. They suffer the same fate as everything on the street: neglect, graffiti, discoloration. The plus side is, they can be repainted, touched up, even altered, and in this respect they resemble a blackboard more closely than an oil painting. If the artist so desires, he or she can have the mural keep pace with the times, updating the images and the concept like a newspaper.

Few mural artists go so far as this, but many spend at least some of their time on upkeep, washing and cleaning off the inevitable graffiti, repainting and touching-up the faded areas. Most artists are aware that, exposed as it is to the elements, both human and natural, there is a limited life-expectancy for any mural. At best, with lightfast pigments, perfect priming and protective coating, a mural will last thirty years–always assuming that the building will stay up that long, a serious consideration in Los Angeles. "I've always thought of painted murals as contemporary statements that could last about ten years outside," wrote David Botello, but "with good wall-preparation, generous amounts of compatible paint and sealer, periodic inspection and touch-up, I hope they can last a lot longer."

The chief enemy of murals so far has been graffiti. Sometimes it is a rival gang leaving their *placa* on another gang's wall. Someone paints a moustache on Marilyn Monroe in a Hollywood mural. The damage may be inspired by more than mischief. Thomas Suriya once found a bullet in his mural where someone had shot at Henry Fonda. A black man in Richard Wyatt's freeway Olympic mural *The Spectators* was disfigured by yellow paint. A gay-oriented mural entitled *Spirit of our Future* had comments about AIDS sprayed over it.

Ironically, the resins spread over the mural to protect them from attacks such as these have often proved incompatible with the underlying paint, and in the last decade, anti-graffiti coverings have caused more serious damage than the vandalism they were meant to prevent. Ismael Cazarea lost an entire mural in a matter of a few years, and David Botello watched his first solo mural, *Dreams of Flight*, peel and flake despite the assurances of the manufacturer who had provided a 'protective resin'.

The wall on which Kent Twitchell painted Lita Albuquerque, part of his *Seventh Street Altar Piece*, was damp, he knew, so he used acrylic emulsions rather than solutions to let the mural breathe. The city covered the finished piece with an acrylic solution that dried impermeable, and water has already begun to fog the hands.

Some artists, notably Willie Herrón, have solved the problem of graffiti, at least, by leaving a space in their murals for the inevitable *placas*, incorporating them in the composition.

David Botello writes in *Community Murals:* "The best protection against graffiti is a good, beautiful piece of art that represents and speaks to the community in images that it understands. Some people look for easy answers in protective washable coatings, but the sun and rain will eventually do in any painted mural."

Gently fading murals are spread all around Los Angeles, slowly weathering, like the walls of the LA Fine Arts Squad, whose thin layers of cheap oil paint never could have lasted, nostalgic reminders of a past decade of glory.

Occasionally murals fall prey, not to time, but to the profit motive. In 1982 a motel was built in front of Kent Twitchell's *Freeway Lady*, leaving only her head and shoulders visible: in December 1986 the owner of the building allowed a wall-leasing company to whitewash over the mural, putting in its place the words "Your Ad Here" and a phone number. The company's telephone never stopped ringing for the next few days with outraged Angelenos complaining that their beloved "Freeway Lady" had been taken from them.

The public reaction to the disappearance of *The Freeway Lady* helped to galvanize the LA art community into forming the Los Angeles Mural Conservancy, a consortium of three local artists' groups which undertook to register and maintain murals throughout the Los Angeles area. Their first challenge came only six weeks after *The Freeway Lady* disappeared, when the new owner of a Hollywood building painted out Twitchell's 1971 *Strother Martin* to comply with insurance regulations. Twitchell is now in the process of restoring it with the help of the Conservancy. Meanwhile, only the eyes of *Freeway Lady* are still visible, peering out from her white covering.

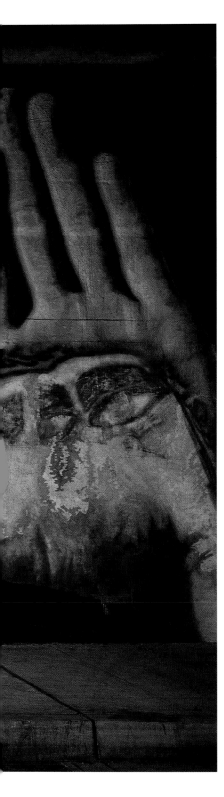

Portrait of the artist Jim Morphesis, one half of Kent Twitchell's *Seventh Street Altarpiece*. "Why hands? The artist views the city through his hands as if framing it. And it's also a sign of vulnerability; open hands mean no weapons." Morphesis's palms are scarred by spray-paint and fogged with moisture

LA Fine Arts Squad's classic *Isle of California*, a vision of a shattered freeway remnant set against the backdrop of Death Valley. Its thin layers of oil paint have faded in the strong LA sun

27

Birth of a mural: *Baseball.*
A crew of painters projects
the image in vertical
swaths the width of the
mobile scaffold. Time is
money: commercial murals
go up fast. Barely a month
has passed and the five-
storey-high mural is
completed. A wall this size
can cost several thousand
dollars a month to rent,

besides the cost of putting the
painting on the wall. Nike was
one of the first companies in
Los Angeles to adopt murals–
whole walls with no ad copy–
as vehicles for advertising.
"LA is a mobile town. Murals
were a natural way to reach
people," says Jeff Gorman,
former copywriter at Chiat-
Day, the ad agency responsible
for Nike's move to murals

29

Going to the Olympics, a freeway mural by Frank Romero

SCENE THROUGH THE WINDSHIELD

LA Freeway Kids by Glenna Boltuch-Avila. The youngsters are all children she knows. She spent a year on the mural, 6 months in the studio and 5 at the wall, painting only on weekends when the traffic was lighter. "It was a little bit nerve-wracking out there; it's hard to concentrate on your art in that setting."

Faces and figures rise up from the underpass, surreal scenes whizz by on off-ramps and junctions. Seven cars long, six children frolic beside the Hollywood Freeway. These *Freeway Kids* were an Olympic commission in downtown LA. The Children's Museum lies behind them, and the artist, Glenna Boltuch-Avila, is a former director of the Citywide Murals Project, responsible for over 250 community-orientated murals in LA County. In the city of the motor car, the windshield becomes the entree to a many-faceted, free art show: Madonnas glowing in golden afternoon colors; floating classical debris, post-modern art, post-technological society. Two artists, Jim Morphesis and Lita Albuquerque, face each other across 12 lanes of incessant traffic on the Seventh Street Underpass, Harbor Freeway. Lillian Bronson, a bit actor for many years, breathed a softness over the Hollywood Freeway that earned her the name "The Freeway Lady". And that's just for starters . . .

"Everybody's driving, and everyone's in a rush," says Alonzo Davis. John Wehrle uses the speed of cars to his advantage in *Galileo, Jupiter, Apollo*: "I wanted the illusion of the architecture orbiting in space as you drive by." Chugging along beside the real traffic, Frank Romero's buzzing cartoon-cars are like an alternative magical freeway. At 55 miles per hour, these sedans from the forties be-bop past graffiti-like palms to a more carefree beat. The "Freeway Kids" transmit a sense of joy and abandon to the most jaded commuter. Judith Hernandez's warm yellows in *Recuerdos de Ayer, Suenos de mañana* shine out two blocks away. The electric colors of Willie Herrón's *Luchas del Mundo* light up the concrete city.

Even on the streets and the highways of LA the viewer will not always be in motion. Jane Golden painted her turn-of-the-century beachfront scene on the ruins of the old Sorrento Hotel on the Pacific Coast Highway to be "something serene and romantic" for all those drivers stuck in traffic.

Eyes by Ruben Brucelyn, a former Chicano gang-member (painted left, beside his pastor), and Kent Twitchell. Twitchell's influence is seen in the side light, the frank expressions

GROW WITH THE OLYMPICS

SPEED
LIMIT
55

James, an enigmatic
scene in downtown LA
by Richard Wyatt

Recuerdos de Ayer, Suenos de Mañana ("Memories of Yesterday, Dreams of Tomorrow"). A golden Madonna painted by Judith Hernandez as part of the 1981 bicentennial celebrations for the city. Note the clever use of space to fit the head onto the wall

Above left: **Sorrento Ruins by Jane Golden, painted as "something serene and romantic for all those people stuck in traffic" on the Pacific Coast Highway**

Below left: **John Wehrle's Galileo, Jupiter, Apollo gives a different sense of serenity to motorists driving through the Freeway 101 'Slot' downtown**

Willie Herrón's Luchas del Mundo ("Struggles of the World"). Neon karatekas fight it out against a backdrop of a Mission facade and flying Olympic banners

THE 23RD OLYMPIAD WELCOMES YOU

Walls ablaze with color and movement honor the athletic champions of the world. The Los Angeles Olympic Organizing Committee planned to line the marathon route with murals as part of the Olympics Arts Festival, but the route eventually chosen passed through a number of low-visibility secondary streets. The murals project could not have been realized had not the Californian Department of Transport stepped in with an offer of sites on the major freeways. Ten artists, representing a wide spectrum of ethnic backgrounds, were selected for their previous mural work in the city. Willie Herrón, Frank Romero and Judy Baca came out of the East LA mural movement of the seventies. Alonzo Davis, Richard Wyatt and Roderick Sykes were Black muralists; Terry Schoonhoven, Kent Twitchell and John Wehrle came out of the 'fine arts' school of LA murals; Glenna Boltuch-Avila—who chose to paint her "Freeway Kids" opposite the Children's Museum—had been director of the Citywide Murals Project.

To accomplish their murals the artists worked for hundreds of hours in an extremely hostile environment, fighting the noise, the constant wind, the high carbon-monoxide levels. The stipend usually covered only the cost of materials. The completed murals are labors of love, and worthy of the city. Spread over hundreds of square yards of freeway walls, they are visible for only seconds at a time—except for the lucky few each day stuck in rush-hour traffic and able to appreciate them fully.

Other, 'unofficial' murals also were created as mementos of those two weeks in 1984 when the world watched Los Angeles. The East Los Streetscapers' *El Nuevo Fuego* ("The New Fire") on the Victor Building (p. 40) combined the notions of the Olympic flame and the ancient Aztec fire-ceremony. Nike produced monumental portraits of Alberto Salazar and Joan Benoit, the winning marathoners, close to the Olympic Coliseum. And opposite the Coliseum, the 'Queen of Angels' welcomed the world to the Olympics in a massive 132 foot by 43 foot mural (right). Los Angeles had recognized the place of murals in its tradition, and all the world saw that LA was indeed the capital of the big picture.

Following pages
Sprinter Valerie Brisco-Hooks is first to the tape in East Los Streetscapers' *El Nuevo Fuego* on the downtown Victor Building. Joan Benoit wins a marathon in photorealist style on a Nike mural close to the Coliseum

Exposition Park Welcomes the World **by Joe Gonzales and Robert Arenivar, completed by 20 local highschool students**

Previous page
Sports by Ruben Brucelyn makes good use of walls and stairways at Echo Park

Las Olimpiadas **by Frank Martinez, on a wall of the East Los Angeles College, the Field Hockey Site. Masked figures represent the Olympic Arts Festival**

We Shall Never Forget. A crowded memento of the Olympics on the wall of a downtown motel

45

East Los Streetscapers'
Payless Shoes Commission,
Corrido de Boyle Heights.
"Corrido" is a ballad in the
distinctive *norteña* (northern)
Mexican style. The
composition borrows from
both comics and classics:
"We like Rubens, he invented
movement," says Healy

Women's Community Center
birthday party by Ann Wolken

East LA is a world unto itself, and its murals are unique. The population is composed almost entirely of Mexican-Americans—Chicanos, as they often call themselves. For California was Spanish long before it was American. This century, hundreds of thousands of Mexicans crossed the border to seek work in the fields and towns of California, and though upwards of 300,000 were deported in the early 1930s in the wake of the Great Depression, great numbers remained, and the area known as East Los Angeles became their enclave.

There has always been a tradition of decorative art in Mexican culture, but few of the young artists who took to the walls in the seventies knew of their famous predecessors; when they began they were more familiar with Superman than with Siqueiros. Soon, however, pictures of Aztec warriors and Aztec temples, faces and figures taken from Mayan statuary, began to sprout on the walls of the *barrios*. Central meeting centers for artists, such as the Goez and Mechicano studios, flourished; artists formed themselves into groups and associations, such as Los Four or ASCO. Many people were involved in the creation of a mural, not only artists; the mural site became a town meeting, and everyone from children to octogenarians took part. Several murals that sprang up were painted by *pachucos* (members of a "bandilla", or gang) who, organized by an artists—sometimes an ex-gang member himself—were able to channel their anger, talent and energy on to the walls of a local market.

The experience of the Chicano murals led to the establishment of a tradition of community murals in Los Angeles. Korean, Jewish, Black, Gay, Women's and Men's Community Centers now have community murals detailing their history and self-images. Today, many of these murals are additions to the urban scenery which carry a softer message, like a scene of women of many races celebrating together. These official community murals are funded by local businesses and overseen by elected committees, but on the sides of local markets throughout the *barrios* unauthorized and unsanctioned community murals continue to appear with images of homeboys, lowrider cars, Madonnas, Christs, and graphic pleas for an end to gang violence. That's how it all began . . .

49

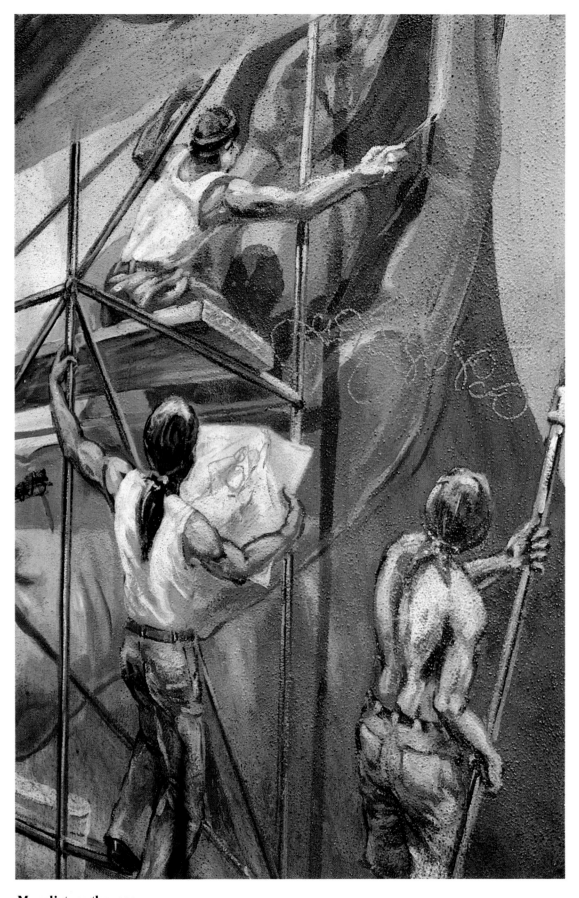

Right: **Technological Man**, a Venice mural from the seventies by Joe Bravo

Below right: **Father Hidalgo Rang the Bell of Dolores**. The outbreak of the Mexican Revolution in 1810, depicted in the Placita de Dolores, LA's historic central downtown area

Muralists as they see themselves: a detail from *Chicano Time Trip* **by Los Dos Streetscapers**

Chevy by Denis Fitzpatrick, a homage to the ultimate Lowrider Car. Painted in 1975, it is untouched by graffiti—a revered icon

Homeboy, Homegirl by John Valadez. Side of a market in East LA

Nurturance by Ann Thiermann, "This wall is a labor of love," reads the Spanish version of the message painted on the wall of the Venice Health Center. The telephone number is for SPARC, which once administered the program

Peace Through War, a cartoon-mural off Hollywood Boulevard makes a political statement. *End Barrio Warfare* (below) is a plea to remember all the "beautiful homeboys" who grew up in East LA and died in the gang wars

Spirit of our Future, a scene
from the fanciful mural
designed by Carlos Callejo
and E. Rodriguez, and
painted by the local
community. Each May, the
Sunset Junction Fair
depicted here celebrates the
ethnic mix of LA, and
especially its gay and lesbian
communities. In the section
Discover the East Side a
"homeboy" slides down a
rainbow-ribbon, crossing
over the LA basin as it was
before habitation

56

DISCOVER THE EAST SIDE

A blues musician and singer *(far right)* on ***Inner City Cultural Center***, a 200-foot-long montage mural by Roberto (Tito) Delgado

Ofrenda Maya ("Mayan Offering") on the City Terrace Library, designed by the late Robert Arenivar, one of the talented unsung artists of the East LA mural movement. The tiles are made in the local Goez studios

Willie Herrón's art deco vision of Chicanos streaming towards the future, *La Doliente de Hidalgo*, on the side of a local market

Estrada Courts

Dozens of murals transform Estrada Courts into a lively family environment. In 1974 Charles "Gato" Felix, a self-taught muralist, undertook to co-ordinate youths and gang-members in a unique project to cover 80 two-storey walls in Estrada Courts, a large Los Angeles housing development. Forty big murals were completed and an immense variety of smaller ones. The subjects span the whole range, from outright agit prop through history to abstract paintings.

Large murals led on to
smaller murals at Estrada
Courts, until they appeared
on any blank surface, like
this one on a simple low wall

Mexican motifs and lime
helados

Living with murals: the housing development becomes a magical wonderland. *Left:* a Mexican festival. The murals are a dozen years old now, and the LA sun has taken its toll

67

The children of Crossroads
School, Santa Monica, meet
and eat outside in 'the alley',
where they have created their
ideal 'student lounge'

Kids' stuff: vibrant design at Crossroads School, Santa Monica

Mexican muralist Josefina Quesada was brought in to restore the 1932 Siqueiros mural *American Tropical*, whitewashed over to cover a message then considered politically unpopular. She never got to restore the mural by the great Mexican muralist; instead, she completed several walls of her own, including this one, *Read*, on the side of the Anthony Quinn Public Library

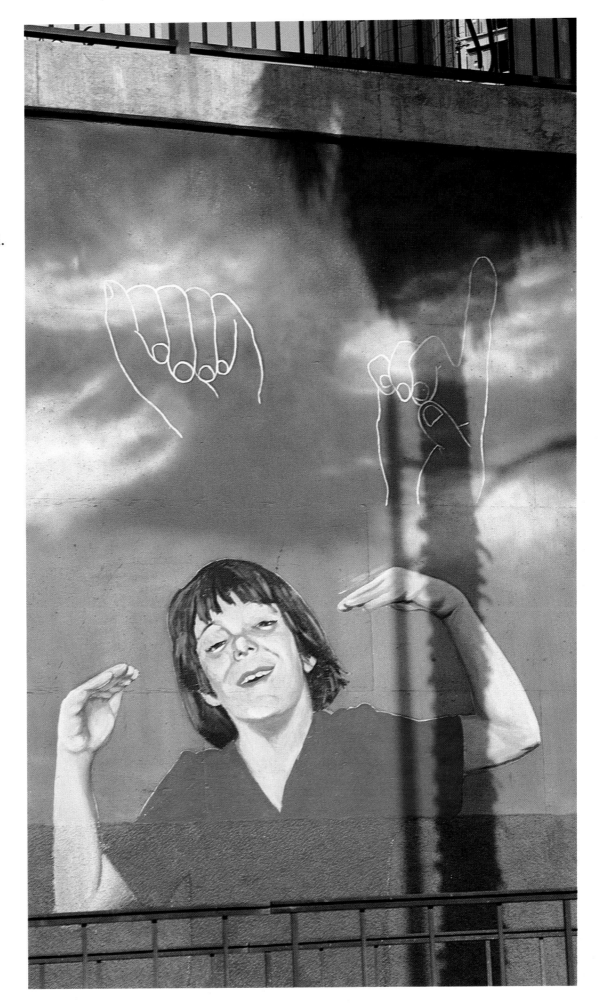

Signing. A deaf child signs 'hope' on this freeway mural. Margaret Garcia worked with a crew of five deaf teenagers on a summer employment program

71

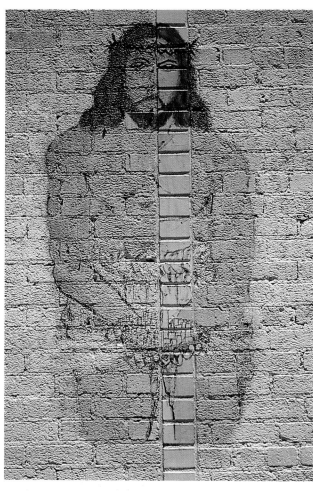

DEDICATED TO
RONNIE L. LLANES
DWAYNE M. WALKER

Left: **Neighborhood Christ with Roses,** mural in the Pico-Union area. *Below left:* dedication to fallen gang member. *Below:* in *Choices* a "homeboy" turns to crime and pays for it in jail: a mural designed by Daniel Martinez and painted by the members of the Playboys Gang whose zoot-suited rabbit mascot watches at left

72

Walls of salvation

On the walls of the *barrio* as in the churches of Mexico the Madonna appears as the Virgin of Guadalupe. Legend is that in December 1531 a simple Indian peasant by the name of Juan Diego had a vision of Mary, who told him to go to the Bishop of Mexico City and command him to build a cathedral for her. The Bishop heard Diego's message, but asked to be given a sign. Three days later Diego saw the Holy Mother again. She told him to gather roses, which she arranged on his "tilma," a piece of clothing he was wearing, saying he should carry them to the Bishop without disturbing their arrangement. When the tilma was opened a glowing likeness of the Virgin appeared on the piece of native cloth. The cathedral was built, and the image came to be known as the Virgin of Guadalupe—for Mexicans and Chicanos their own dark Madonna.

Left: **The Virgin of Guadalupe on a wall in the Highland Park area.** *Right:* **The Madonna on a building at Estrada Courts**

WALLS THAT SING SAGAS

Los Angeles has a rich and diverse history, a tapestry of the many different ethnic groups that settled here. But for the most part, this history is neglected or forgotten. Los Angeles is a city which prides itself on living in the present and looking only to the future. The pride in cultural identity that blossomed in the sixties, however, sparked a need among the different communities to teach their members their common past—or to create one. Chicano muralists used Aztec symbols in their murals, while Black muralists such as Alonzo Davis were often inspired by African motifs. Later on, these poetic and mythic themes were joined by more factual murals portraying the recorded events of Los Angeles' two hundred years of existence.

The Fairfax Community Mural was conceived to help revitalize the heart of the LA Jewish community, the Fairfax district. Muralist Art Mortimer used a collage of old photographs to portray the events of each epoch. He hired two artist-assistants, organized a corps of volunteers of ages ranging from 14 to 74 years, laid on classes in the local highschool, divided his workers into teams, and set about choosing 35 photographic scenes to be rendered in monochrome from among the thousands of archival photos collected.

The three-part mural *La Vida Breve* tells the story of the area's history through the eyes of an old man explaining to his youthful student how the hillsides have changed over the years—from the bucolic past to the polluted present. It has the distinction of being the only mural in Los Angeles to have been blessed by a bishop. Jane Golden's *Early Ocean Park* evokes the atmosphere of "the old days" in a single scene.

The Streetscapers' *Moonscapes* takes a more fanciful view of the past, with its pictures of Einstein and a Mayan astronomer. But undoubtedly the most ambitious in scope and purpose of all the history murals is the series of scenes—half-a-mile long and still growing—begun by Judy Baca in 1976, and now known as "The Great Wall" of Los Angeles.

76

Early Ocean Park by Jane Golden depicts a scene in the 1920s. "I discovered the Santa Monica Pier had been torn down and I thought it would be a really nice gesture to put it up again for the people."

Los Angeles at the turn of the century: the second scene of a three-part history entitled *La Vida Breve de Alfonso Fulano* ("The Short Life of Joe Everyman"). A Goez commission designed by Robert Arenivar

Opposite: two views of *Hester Street* by Jane Golden. Many members of the LA Jewish community came from New York. Hester Street, lower East Side, evokes the immigrant past for them

The Los Dos Streetscapers give us a cruise through space and time on the walls of the Department of Motor Vehicles in Culver City. *Left: Moonscapes'* Mayan astronomer hangs in a space-time grid; *right:* **Einstein pedals down a time-line.** *Below:* **"space figures" beneath a total eclipse. Their meaning? "We're not really sure what they are," says Healy. "People still come up to us with their own explanations."**

The Fairfax Community Mural. 35 images on 7 panels tell the story of the LA Jewish community

Below: **Beginnings 1841-1880.** LA's first permanent synagogue is flanked by its first rabbi and four generations of the family of the congregation's first president. *Bottom:* **Fairfax Today, 1985**, taken from photographs by Bill Aron shows typical street-scenes: buying fruit at an open-air stall, orthodox Jews, a bus bench and a group of muralists taking a break from their work

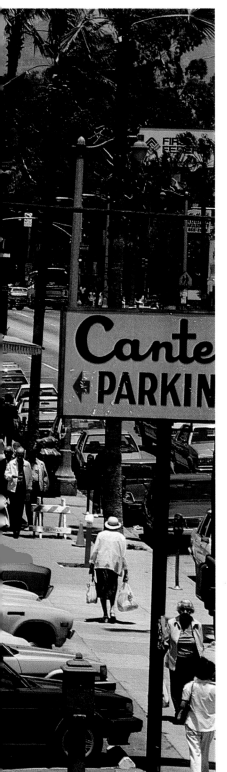

83

A Hogarthian picture of the dangers of alcohol by Ann Thiermann, painted on the side of a rehabilitation center, Clare, in Santa Monica

DUSTBOWL: Faulty agriculture in the 1930s resulted in disastrous soil erosion. Especially hard hit was Oklahoma. The exodus of 'Okies' who headed for California was the theme of a famous novel, John Steinbeck's *The Grapes of Wrath*

WORLD WAR II: Six years of war are compressed into a single set of images

JEWISH ARTS AND SCIENCE: Einstein holds an atomic fireball. In the background, an Escher-like image of swords transforming themselves into plowshares

DUSTBOWL REFUGEES

WORLD WAR II

The Great Wall

Judy Baca was originally approached by the US Army Corps of Engineers in 1976 to paint a couple of murals in an out-of-the-way flood control channel in Coldwater Canyon. Their concrete engineering had created a blighted area, and their Aesthetic Planning Division felt that one or two murals would add a touch of color and beauty to the surroundings. Little did they, or she, know that it would grow into an annual project involving, thus far, 250 teenagers, 75,000 hours of work, 50 supervising artists and 700 gallons of paint. Now the wall along one side of this concrete channel in "The Valley" (San Fernando Valley) boasts the longest mural in the world. It is 2,500 feet long by 13 feet high.

Baca chose to portray the little-known ethnic history of Los Angeles, and sought out historians to establish the themes of an era. The first thumbnail sketches were submitted to poets and artists—"people who speak in metaphor", as Baca put it—and final revisions were undertaken with the help of "living historians"—those who had actually lived through the events depicted. The result is as narrative in which history is seen as a range of events and also attitudes.

The environment in the flood-control basin is a hostile one. Sandbags keep back the water which continues to trickle even in summer when the crews are working. One year a flash flood washed away a scaffold and $20,000

worth of equipment. Within a week it was set up again. Temperatures at noon rise above 100 degrees Farenheit.

The teenagers who form these crews represent the LA population. They are chosen from a wide variety of ethnic backgrounds, and many are from poor neighborhoods. "We actually had to teach some of them to use rulers," says Baca.

Every 350-foot section is completed by five teenagers under the direction of one artist. Care is taken to mix up the tasks, so that no group identifies with a particular

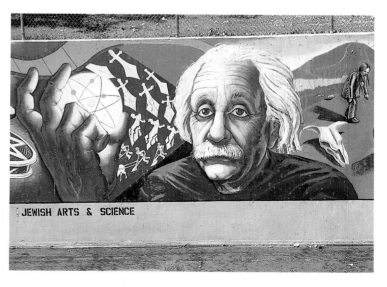

JEWISH ARTS & SCIENCE

86

FAT, SCREAMING BABY: A gargantuan child represents the postwar "baby-boom". Black soldiers peer into the living-room, denied access to the post-war suburbs. "We found our sense of humor in the fifties," says Judy Baca

THE RED SCARE: Senator McCarthy casts a long shadow over Hollywood. In 1947 the House Committee on Un-American Activities investigated the loyalty of 19 actors, directors and writers. Ten were found guilty of contempt, and jailed

CIVIL RIGHTS: Paul Robeson is in the foreground. At right, Rosa Park refuses to give up her seat at the front of the bus. It is the early sixties, and the start of the fight for Civil Rights

area of the wall. The area is sand- and water-blasted, then 'primed out' with an undercoat of white gesso. The wall is chalk-lined into grids, and the cartoon is projected on to the wall using painted blue lines, one grid at a time. Then a magenta undercoat is applied which serves two purposes: to blend the colors to come, and to color the inevitable 'holidays' (air bubbles bursting in the cement), so they come up magenta rather than white.

Each panel has its own base-color, which is applied broadly; then the dark colors are filled in, and the highlight colors come last. "Scumbling," a painting technique using as half-dry brush, allows the colors from

underneath to come through. In 1977 Baca studied with the renowned muralist Siqueiros at his workshop in Mexico. His concept of the "punto de oro" (point of gold) ratio invigorated her designs with energetic triangular figures that give the panels an underlying geometric unity.

A sombre view of much of the modern age lightens as the mural moves into the post-War epoch. "We found our sense of humour in the fifties," says Baca. In the next few years the Great Wall will catch up to the present, and engage in visions of the future.

The Great Wall is a work of art with a strong conceptual basis—that of racial and social harmony. In the project's 10 years to date, over 500 volunteers from disparate backgrounds worked, played and co-operated with one another in its realization. Without the focus of the wall, these individuals—mostly teens—would have remained isolated in their geographically separate communities, unaware of the wealth of cultural variety that surrounds them. In this sense, the Great Wall is far more than a series of murals in a flood control channel. It is a tool for multicultural co-operation. Baca refers to the project as a "tolerance-matrix", for its creation is a mirror of the manner in which the city developed in the past, and a model for Los Angeles in the year 2000—and beyond.

87

ESCAPE FROM THE GALLERIES

"I tried the galleries but I was too dramatic. So I took to the streets," remembers Rozzel Sykes about a 1961 painting. "We didn't call them murals in the beginning," says Art Mortimer, "we called them wall-paintings. We were doing art outside—using the city as our canvas." But often the impulse to paint murals was political, an anti-establishment activity. In by-passing the galleries the painters made their art unconditionally available to everyone. They started putting art into public spaces so as to communicate, and soon they were reaching tens of thousands. For many people, even if they only catch a fleeting glance, these murals are the only original art they will ever get to see.

In the late sixties, Vic Henderson and Terry Schoonhoven painted a mural on the side of Henderson's Venice Studio. The scene was a replica of what the observer saw with his back to the mural; and even before completing it, they had moved furniture into the vacant lot beside the mural and made it into a living-room. "We felt we had seized the land around the mural," Henderson observed. Schoonhoven's *Cityscape* (p.2) also mirrors the section of downtown facing the mural, but with the addition of the Parthenon and the AT&T Building with its top sheared off. "It's a surreal stage-set, the scene after a quiet cataclysm," is how Schoonhoven describes the work.

While Chicano artists worked with the community—a mural was a neighborhood event with everyone, especially teenagers, participating in the painting—Anglo (white) muralists generally worked alone, as artists on behalf of the community. The result, however, was the same: the wall and the space around it, once painted, ceased to be perceived as private property or blank neutral space.

Eventually Henderson and Schoonhoven joined with two other artists to form the LA Fine Arts Squad. The art critics and the galleries didn't know what to make of this public art. The Chicano art could be seen as "folk art," and then dismissed with a few comments about "mixed iconographies." The art that appeared on the walls of Venice was at least as good technically as that found in the major galleries, and much funnier. But it couldn't be bought and sold. So the art establishment ignored it. "Murals have had a real struggle with legitimacy,"

Kent Twitchell notes. The legitimacy was certainly slow in coming, but it arrived none the less. Paul Harter, owner of the Victor Building, had commissioned Twitchell as early as '72 to do *Bride and Groom* (p. 102), a stunning monochrome study of five-storey-high ordinary people. By 1984 there were six other major murals painted by Latino artists who had made a name for themselves as early muralists in the *barrios*. Each one is a study in individual style and technique.

88

Botticelli's Venus takes to the Boardwalk in *Venice on the Half Shell* by R. Cronk. *Below:* Venice Beach, the rollerskating capital of the world. The mural depicts the scene it faces, and includes the varied beachfront population

89

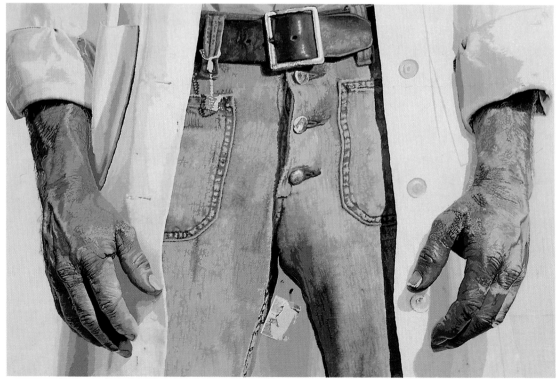

Holy Trinity with the Virgin, Kent Twitchell's Master's project at Otis Parsons Art Institute. The model for the Virgin was actress Jan Clayton, who represented motherhood for a generation of Americans—she played the mother on the fifties TV program "Lassie". The Son, Bud Anderson, was the teenage son in the fifties TV classic "Father Knows Best". He wears a watch fob, hinting at the Second Coming. "The white lab coats represent the Wise Men's robes, but also gives them the sense of a fifties science fiction movie," says Twitchell. Actor Clayton Moore, "The Lone Ranger", appears as God the Father. A finger of the Virgin's right

hand makes the one emotional gesture to be found in any work by Twitchell. And the space between father and son? "When somebody shows me what the Holy Spirit looks like, I'll paint it."

Following page: Twitchell's *Gary Lloyd Monument,* painted on the side of City Sea Foods, downtown. "I must have taken 150 photographs to get the exact expression—strong, but accepting."

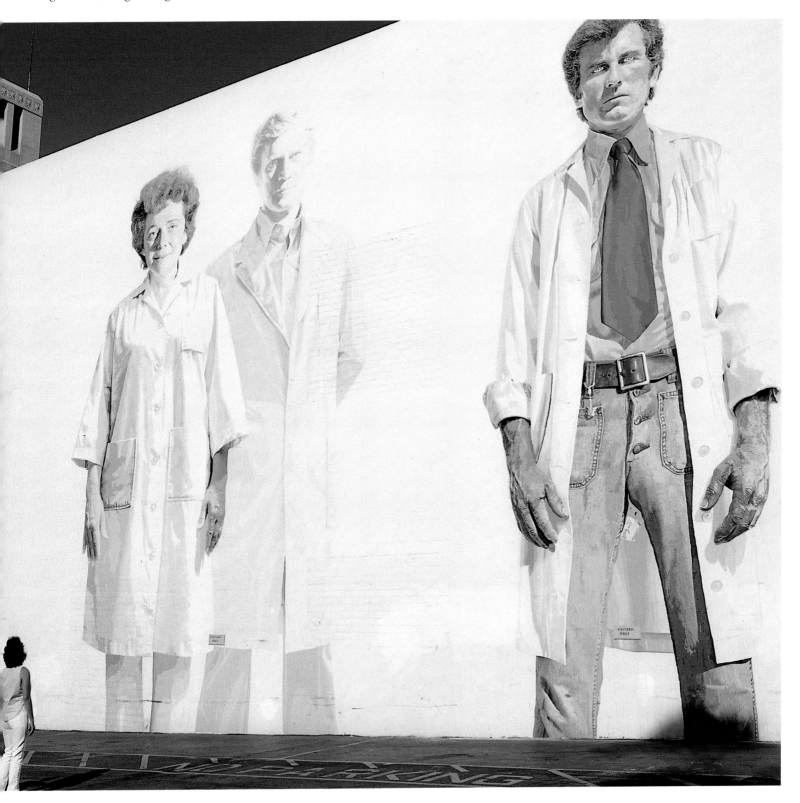

91

Previous page
A section of the Streetscapers' 200-foot-long mural *Filling Up On Ancient Energies*

Putting the finishing touches to Thierry Bernard's *Miss Liberty* in time for her July 4th centenary celebrations

97

Jane Golden's *John Muir Forest*—redwoods on a school in Santa Monica

Following pages
Bride and Groom (Monarch) and *El Nuevo Fuego*. North wall of the Victor Building, downtown

Bride and Groom. Kent Twitchell painted his bridal couple in monochrome blues to set it apart from advertising images. He painted the Groom—the owner of a bridal clothing factory—in 1973, then spent the next three years, on and off, painting the Bride while still a student at Otis Parsons Art Institute. "I took a slide of the wall from a distance so I didn't have any three-point perspective to contend with, and then I projected the building on a wall in my studio, and planned her around the constraints of the windows." He painted most of the mural at night, working by the light of a single electric lamp, so as to avoid paying for daytime parking in the lot below

102

Anthony Quinn dances, Zorba-like, seven stories high and 60 feet across from fingertip to fingertip. Eloy Torrez calls his work the *Pope of Broadway* in a reference to the actor's career and to the location of the Victor Building: the main foyer, pictured, opens on to Broadway

Nino y Caballo ("Boy and Horse"), painted by Frank Romero in graffiti-style

103

Enticing the customer

Flowers, pets, fruits and people decorate shops and restaurants in every corner of the city. Roses bloom six feet high on a café, a cheetah takes over the front of a clothing store. In East LA, murals often depict the wares offered, from cabbages to parrots. The variety is endless—cartoons, photorealism, wallpaper-designs—fantasies of all descriptions . . .

Left: **Art Mortimer took a twenty dollar bill as model for his shop front in Venice Beach, Roller Skates of America.** *Below:* **Airborne commandos advance on Sunset Boulevard, front of Surplus Value Centre**

Style on Omni Stereo, an electronics store front, downtown

106

The proud shopowner with one of his wares in front of a naive Noah's Ark, Elias Pet Shop in East LA

Front of the Cinco de Mayo Market in East LA, named after the Mexican national holiday

Brandelli's Brig is muralist Art Mortimer's personal favorite, a photorealistic mural-within-a-mural on the side of the ex-boxer's bar which it portrays. He designed the *trompe l'oeil* for passing motorists "to jog their awareness a little bit, and so give them a bit of a different perspective on the rest of their lives."

107

Roses cluster round the door of the Rose Café, a popular Venice rendez-vous. The store *Cactus on Rose* (*right*) is no longer selling cactuses on Rose Avenue, but the mural lives on

A deer chews a ginseng root on the wall of an Acupuncture Clinic in Koreatown. *Below right:* Chinese and Korean ideograms figure on a Mexican restaurant, El Jarrito, over a Mayan jungle-scene

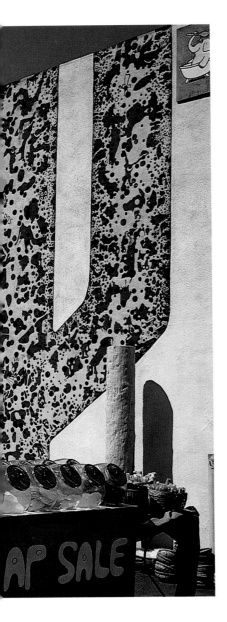

Below: Cheetah-motif on 'A-Zoo', a clothing-store for surfers in Venice Beach. The design took Dyan Brenneison just one day to complete

Bottom: John Garrett's design on the side of a bookstore, Silverlake

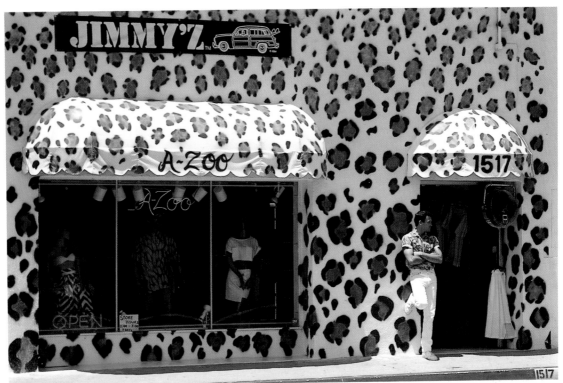

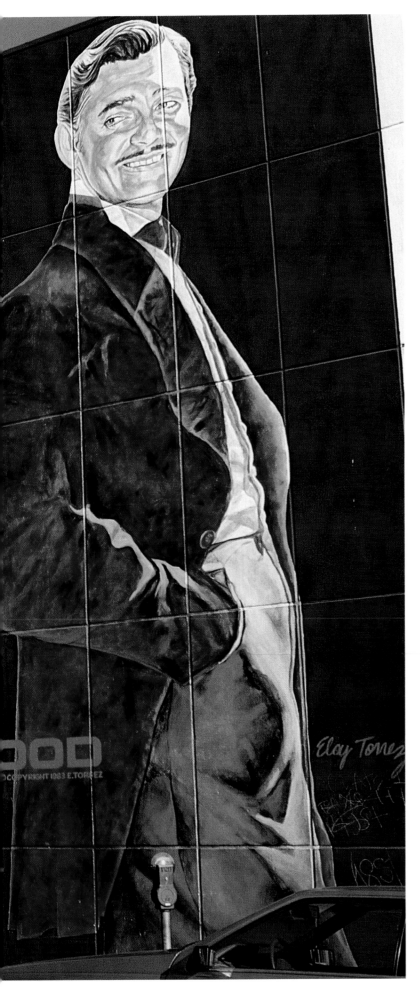

Legends of Hollywood—
Bogart, Astaire, Bette Davis, James Dean and Clark Gable—high over Hollywood Boulevard in a mural by Eloy Torrez. *Below:* **Monroe and Bogart**

THE STARS MAKE IT BIG

Other cities have symbols for which they are famous: a lady with a torch, perhaps, or a mermaid on a rock. Los Angeles has a sign. Fifty feet high and visible for many miles, it is a giant's signature, the letters of which form the word HOLLYWOOD. From well above the house-line in the Hollywood Hills, these letters look down over Hollywood Boulevard. Hollywood gave the world a set of new global mythic heroes. Now the stars appear on the walls of the town that made them legends.

Steve McQueen was Kent Twitchell's first large-scale mural, painted on a friend's house in 1971. McQueen himself was unaware of its existence until he chanced to pass by it on his motorcycle one day, a couple of years after its completion.

He was pleased with it, as is Four-Star International Pictures who own his films. In 1987 they donated $1000 to the Mural Conservancy towards the upkeep of this classic mural.

Thomas Suriya's first mural, *You Are The Star*, is now a Hollywood landmark. He presented the idea for it to the shopowner, Michael Attie, who paid him in room and

111

board, plus $500 to supplement a small stipend from the city.

"I knew that if this ever managed to get on to the wall there would be enough attention, because of the magnitude of the concept and its location; that I would have a foot in the door." He was right. He has since received several other mural commissions around Los Angeles. "Graffiti? They paint moustaches on Monroe, Taylor and Bacall all the time. Someone tried to shoot Henry Fonda once. I dug the slug out myself."

AMTV. **Celebrities on the bus bench–"Mingle with the Stars at the Hollywood Wax Museum"**

Kent Twitchell's
Steve McQueen

A solitary *John McEnroe* in a New York setting, Hollywood Boulevard

Ansel Adams, the famous American landscape photographer, observes the traffic in Hollywood from the side of a photo lab. It is ironic that this photorealistic mural is in full color, for Adams himself photographed almost exclusively in black-and-white

115

Thomas Suriya switches the roles. In _You Are The Star_ the Hollywood Legends sit in the darkened cinema watching us

116

Big names of the big picture: Bogart and Monroe, Katherine Hepburn and Spencer Tracy, Paul Newman and Robert Redford as Butch Cassidy and the Sundance Kid

Following pages
Hunt the stars. Do you see: Mae West and Sophia Loren, Mickey Rooney and Judy Garland, Cantinflas, Richard Pryor, Jane Russell, Al Jolson, ET phoning home . . . James Gagney, Jean Harlow, Edward G. Robinson, John Wayne, Burt Lancaster, Ingrid Bergman, Toshiro Mifune, Grace Kelly, Gary Cooper, Errol Flynn, Godzilla, R2D2, King Kong and Dracula. . . . Liz and Dick, Rudolf Valentino, Henry Fonda and daughter Jane as Barbarella, Marlon Brando, Brigitte Bardot, Burt Reynolds and Dolly Parton, Dustin Hoffman, Theda Bara, Mary Pickford and Elvis Presley, various Marx brothers . . .

119

A WILD LIFE

Life-size horses gallop opposite a 600-foot blue wall adorned with gamboling whales and porpoises. Elephants grace a house in Santa Monica. A leopard crouches ready to spring on the side of project housing. Wild life—*real* wild life, that is—is scarcely ever seen in Los Angeles, but murals have come to the city to redress the balance.

Some of the pictures of animals, however, add more than decoration. When Margaret Garcia was commissioned to do a mural for Citywide Mural Projects she was told the subject-matter should be "something of social importance". Garcia chose to cover her wall with two whales. The fate of whales had become a symbol of the destruction of the environment in the seventies; the continuing attack on the species had served to focus conservation activities, and prompted the formation of organizations such as Greenpeace. Garcia's mural reminds us to 'save the whales', and of what we stand to lose.

Hog Heaven is a vision of a porcine paradise, four full city blocks long, a mural painted on the exterior of an abattoir and processing facility in Vernon. The mural was begun in 1957 by Les Grimes, and the work was continued from 1969 by Arno Jordan after Grimes had fallen to his death from the scaffold. Jordan spends 7 months a year, 5 hours a day, on the upkeep of the mural, touching-up, repainting, and designing new panels. "The most difficult area to paint? Why," says Jordan, "that's the wall facing Vernon, where the sidewalk's narrow and cars pass close by the ladders."

Save the Whales by Margaret Garcia and Randy Geraldi

120

121

Two endangered species: an early sixties Cadillac, and blue whales, here in Daniel Alonzo's 600-foot-long *Whale Mural*. Real blue whales are up to 100 foot long: the largest mammals in the world. These are 80 percent scale reductions

Right: **big cat and peacock, side of Estrada Courts project housing**

123

Elephants grace the wall of a private house in Santa Monica. A liberated carousel horse gallops through the surf on Santa Monica beach in *Unbridled (below)* by David Gordon

Hog Heaven, a porcine paradise portrayed on the walls of a packing plant (Farmer John Sausages) in Vernon. Arno Jordan, right, has spent 19 years, 7 months a year, 5 days a week, on its upkeep, using 200-300 gallons of paint a year

**Stanley Young
and Melba Levick**

Photo Shandel/Ackerman

THE MURALS

Listing is by title, followed by artist's name, sponsor where known, location, sector, and page number. Sponsors' initials: see p. 18. CWMP: Citywide Murals Project. LAOOC: Olympic Arts/ Olympic Organizing Committee.

A Different Light *by John Garrett. Commercial. 4014 S. Monica Blvd. Silverlake.* 109

A-Zoo *by Dyan Brenneisen. Commercial. Windward & Pacific. Venice.* 109

AMTV *by Tim Guyer/Dan Fried. Hollywood & Ivar. Hollywood.* 112

Ansel Adams *by Gallery Scope Mural Team. KT Color Lab. S. Monica & Highland. Hollywood.* 115

Baseball *by David Larks. Nike. Exposition & Harbor Fwy (by DMV). Downtown.* 21, 29

Brandelli's Brig *by Art Mortimer. CAC. West Washington & Palms. Venice.* 107

Bride and Groom (Monarch) *by Kent Twitchell. Carlos Ortiz/ Monarch Clothing. Broadway St, 240 (N Wall, Victor Bldg). Downtown.* 20, 100, 102

Cactus on Rose. *Commercial. Rose & 3rd. Venice.* 108

Chevy *by Dennis Fitzpatrick. CWMP. Echo Park & Avalon. Echo Park.* 52

Chicano Time Trip *by Los Dos Streetscapers, D. Botello, W. Healy. Crocker Bank. 2601 Broadway. ELA.* 50

Choices (Playboy Gang) *by Daniel Martinez, Playboy gang members. Community Youth Gang Services. Pico & Fedora. Downtown.* 73

Cinco de Mayo Market. *Commercial. Matthews & 4th. ELA.* 107

Cityscape *by Terry Schoonhoven. LAOOC. Harbor Fwy S & Wilshire Blvd Offramp. Downtown.* 3

Clare (Windows on Alcoholism) *by Ann Thiermann. Clare. Pico & 9th. Santa Monica.* 84-5

Corrido de Boyle Heights *by East Los Streetscapers, D. Botello, W. Healy. Payless Shoes. Brooklyn & Soto. ELA.* 46

Crossroads School *by kids at Crossroads School. Crossroads School. Olympic & 11th. Santa Monica.* 68, 70

Deer and Ginseng (Acupuncture Clinic). *Commercial. Vermont & Olympic. Downtown.* 108

Early Ocean Park *by Jane Golden. CWMP. Ocean Park & Main. Santa Monica.* 77

Ed Ruscha Monument *by Kent Twitchell. CAC, NEA. Hill/10th. Downtown.* 12-17

El Chavo Restaurant. *Commercial. Sunset & Virgil. Echo Park.* 20

El Jarrito (Painted Stairs) *by G. J. Keith, N. Fram, T. Downs. CWMP. Olympic 2700 block. Downtown.* 108

El Nuevo Fuego *by East Los Streetscapers, D. Botello, W. Healy, with George Yepes. Paul D. Harter/Victor Clothing. Victor Bldg. Downtown.* 6, 8, 21, 40, 101

Elias Pet Shop. *Commercial. Brooklyn & Matthews. ELA.* 107

End Barrio Warfare *by ELA Gang. Dozier & Hazard. ELA.* 55

Estrada Courts *by local artists, residents. Olympic & Lorena. ELA.* 4, 62-7, 75, 123

Exposition Park Welcomes the World. *Design R. Arenivar/Dir. Ernie Barnes. Concpt/art dir. Joe Gonzalez. LAOOC, Community Beautification Proj. Coliseum. Downtown.* 39

Eyes *by Ruben Brucelyn, Kent Twitchell. Angelus Temple, local businesses. Glendale Blvd. under Sunset. Echo Park.* 32

Fairfax Community Mural *by A. Mortimer, S. Anaya, P. Fleischman and community members. Youth Dept., Jewish Federated Cncl of Grtr LA, UCHDC, Vitalize Fairfax. 411 N Fairfax.* 82-3

Father Hidalgo Rang the Bell of Dolores *by Eduardo Carillo. Board of Public Works. Placita de Dolores. Downtown.* 51

Filling Up on Ancient Energies *by East Los Streetscapers, D. Botello, W. Healy, G. Yepes. Shell Oil. Soto & Fourth. ELA.* 95

The Freeway Lady (Lillian Bronson) *by Kent Twitchell. CETA. Hollywood Fwy W of Downtown interchange. Downtown* 5

Galileo, Jupiter, Apollo *by John Wehrle. LAOOC. 101 Fwy & Spring St exit. Downtown.* 21, 36

Gary Lloyd Monument *by Kent Twitchell. Donald Kanner, City Sea Foods. 5th & Towne. Downtown.* 9, 10, 93

Going to the Olympics *by Frank Romero. LAOOC. Hollywood Fwy betw. Alameda, Spring St exits. Downtown.* 30

The Great Wall *by Judy Baca, numerous participants and local youth. Community sources, US Army Corps of Engineers, local, state government agencies. Coldwater Canyon. S.F. Valley.* 86-7

Hester Street *by Jane Golden. Bay Cities JCC. S. Monica & 26th St. Santa Monica* 78

Hog Heaven *by Les Grimes, Arno Jordan. Clougherty Packing Plant. Vernon, CA. Vernon.* 126-7

Holy Trinity with the Virgin *by Kent Twitchell. CAC/NEA. Otis Parsons Art Institute. Downtown.* 90-1

Homeboy, Homegirl *by John Valadez. CWMP. 3rd St & Dangler. ELA.* 53

Inner City Cultural Center *by Roberto (Tito) Delgado. CETA. Pico & Vermont. Downtown.* 58-9

Isle of California *by LA Fine Arts Squad, Vic Henderson, Terry Schoonhoven, Jim Frazin. Jody Hormel. Butler & S. Monica. WLA.* 27

James *by Richard Wyatt. LAOOC. Harbor Frwy N & Adams St Underpass. Downtown.* 34

Joan Benoit, *painter Adam Lustig. Nike. Commercial. Opposite Coliseum. Downtown.* 41

John McEnroe, *by David Larks, Adam Lustig. Nike. Hollywood & Vine. Hollywood.* 114

John Muir Woods *by Jane Golden. CETA. Ocean Park & Lincoln. Ocean Park.* 99

La Doliente de Hidalgo *by Willie Herrón. Shopowner. City Terrace & Hazard. ELA.* 1, 61

LA Freeway Kids *by Glenna Boltuch-Avila. LAOOC. 101 Fwy S nr Los Angeles St exit (view Aliso). Downtown.* 32

La Garaghty Lomita *by Willie Herrón. Self-financed. 1416 Miller. ELA.* 25

La Vida Breve de Alfonso Fulano, *designed by Robert Arenivar. Goez commission. Maravilla Housing Development. Mednik Ave & Brooklyn Ave. ELA.* 79

Las Olimpiadas. *Concept, design, execution by Frank Martinez/Proj. dir. Goez Studios. LAOOC. East LA College. ELA.* 21, 44

Legends of Hollywood *by Eloy Torrez. CWMP. Hollywood & Hudson. Hollywood.* 110-11

Luchas del Mundo *by Willie Herrón. LAOOC. 101 Fwy N past Alameda exit (view Commercial St). Downtown.* 37

Miss Liberty (Cadillac Hotel) *by Thierry Bernard. Network Int'l. Venice Boardwalk (nr Rose). Venice.* 97

Moonscapes *by Los Dos Streetscapers, D. Botello, W. Healy. NEA CAC. Washington & Purdue. Mar Vista.* 80-1

Neighborhood Christ with Roses. *Pico (nr Inner City Cultural Center). Downtown.* 72

Nino Y Caballo *by Frank Romero. Paul D. Harter/Victor Clothing. Victor Bldg. Downtown.* 103

Nurturance *(Venice Health Center) by Ann Thiermann. CWMP. Venice & Brenta. Venice.* 54

Ofrenda Maya *(Mayan Offering). Design R. Arenivar/Proj. Director Joe Gonzalez, Goez Studios/ colorist, B. Gonzalez. J. Correla. LA County. City Terrace e & Hazard. ELA.* 20, 59

Omni Stereo *Commercial. Santee & 8th. Downtown.* 106

Peace Through War. *Hollywood & Argyle. Hollywood.* 55

Pope of Broadway *by Eloy Torrez. Paul D. Harter/Victor Clothing. 240 S. Broadway (Victor Bldg). Downtown.* 21, 103

Recuerdos de Ayer, Suenos de Mañana *by Judith Hernandez. City of Los Angeles. Spring & Arcadia. Downtown.* 35

Read *by Josefina Quesada. Chicana Service Action Centre. Anthony Quinn Public Library. Hazard & Brooklyn. ELA.* 70

Roller Skates of America *by Art Mortimer. Commercial. Windward & Pacific. Venice.* 105

Rose Café *by Rene and Renata. Commercial. Rose & Main. Venice.* 108

Save the Whales *by Margaret Garcia, Randy Geraldi. CWMP. Beethoven & Venice. Venice.* 120, 128

Seventh Street Altar Piece *by Kent Twitchell. LAOOC. 7th St Underpass, Harbor Frwy S. Downtown.* 23, 26

Signing *by Margaret Garcia. CWMP, GLAD, Summer Employment. Olympic & 8th. Downtown.* 71

Sorrento Ruins *by Jane Golden. CETA grant. Pacific Coast Highway, S. Monica.* 36

Spirit of our Future *by Carlos Callejo, E. Rodriguez. Sunset Junction Alliance, CWMP. Sunset & Hyperion. Echo Park.* 56

Sports *by Ruben Brucelyn. Morton Ave entr. Echo Park.* 43

Steve McQueen *by Kent Twitchell. Self-financed. Union St & 12th. Downtown.* 20, 113

Surplus Value Centre. *Commercial. Sunset & Hyperion. Silverlake.* 105

Technological Man *by Joe Bravo. CWMP. Pacific & Market. Venice.* 51

Unbridled *by David Gordon. Frederick R. Weisman Foundation. Ocean Park & 4th St Underpass. Ocean Park.* 4, 19, 124

Unity *by Roderick Sykes. LAOCC. Harbor Fwy N, Figueroa St abandoned underpass. Downtown.* 4

Venice on the Half Shell *by R. Cronk. SPARC. Boardwalk (at Windward). Venice.* 88-9

We Shall Never Forget. *Local businesses. Figueroa & 8th. Downtown.* 45

Whale Mural *by Daniel Alonzo. Self-financed. Ocean Park Blvd & 4th St Underpass. Santa Monica.* 122

Women's Community Center *by Ann Wolken. CWMP/CAC. Los Angeles & 3rd. Downtown.* 48

Workers' Mural. *CWMP. Echo Park & Duane. Echo Park.* 20

You Are The Star *by Thomas Suriya. Michael Attie/CWMP. Hollywood & Wilcox. Hollywood.* 116-19

128